GEOGRAPHY QUEST

DEEP-SEA DANGER

JOHN TOWNSEND

QEB Publishing

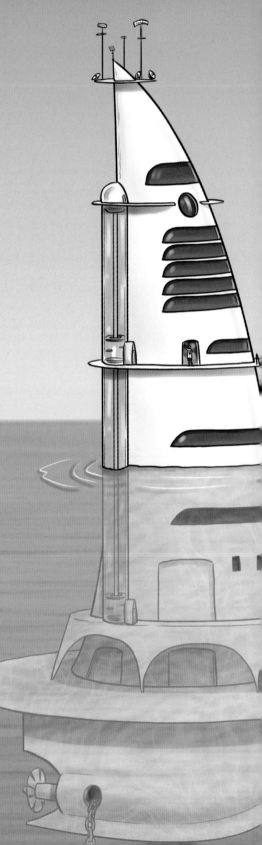

Cover Design: Punch Bowl Design
Illustrator: Tatio Viana
Editor: Claudia Martin
Designer: Carol Davis
QED Project Editors: Ruth Symons
and Carly Madden
QED Project Designer: Rachel Lawston
Editorial Director: Victoria Garrard
Art Director: Laura Roberts-Jensen

First published in the United States by
QEB Publishing, Inc.
3 Wrigley, Suite A
Irvine, CA 92618

www.qed-publishing.co.uk

A CIP record for this book is available from
the Library of Congress.

ISBN 978 1 60992 795 0

Printed in China

Picture credits
Shutterstock: Miguel Angel Salinas Salinas
29, 34; narcisse 8, 42; Talashow 17, 19, 20,
31; Vector 8, 29; whiteisthecolor 7, 9;
Yganko 16, 40.

How to begin your adventure:

Are you ready for an amazing adventure that will test your brain power to the limit—full of mind-bending puzzles, twists, and turns? Then you've come to the right place!

Deep-Sea Danger is no ordinary book—you don't read the pages in order, 1, 2, 3 . . .

Instead you jump forward and backward through the book as you face a series of challenges. Sometimes you may lose your way, but the story will always guide you back to where you need to be.

The story begins on page 4. Straight away, there are questions to answer and problems to overcome. The questions will look something like this:

IF YOU THINK THE CORRECT ANSWER IS A, GO TO PAGE 10

A

IF YOU THINK THE CORRECT ANSWER IS B, GO TO PAGE 18

B

Your task is to solve each problem. If you think the correct answer is A, turn to page 10 and look for the same symbol in red. That's where you will find the next part of the story. If you make the wrong choice, the text will explain where you went wrong and let you have another chance.

The problems in this adventure are about coastal landscapes and the power of the sea. To solve them, you must use your geography skills. To help you, there's a glossary of useful words at the back of the book, starting on page 44.

ARE YOU READY? Turn the page and let your adventure begin!

DEEP-SEA DANGER

You have been summoned to Professor Fustigate's dusty study at the Ocean Explorers Museum. He trembles with excitement as he speaks:

This trunk washed ashore after the pirate ship Shiver Me Timbers sank 300 years ago. Ever since, explorers have tried to find the wreck—but no one knows where it lies.

Yesterday I made a huge discovery: the captain's logbook was hidden in the trunk all along, behind a secret panel. If you can follow its coded clues, it will lead you to the wreck and its treasure.

LOGBOOK

This mission is perfect for a geographer with a boat. That's you!

IF YOU'RE READY TO SET SAIL

TURN TO PAGE 12

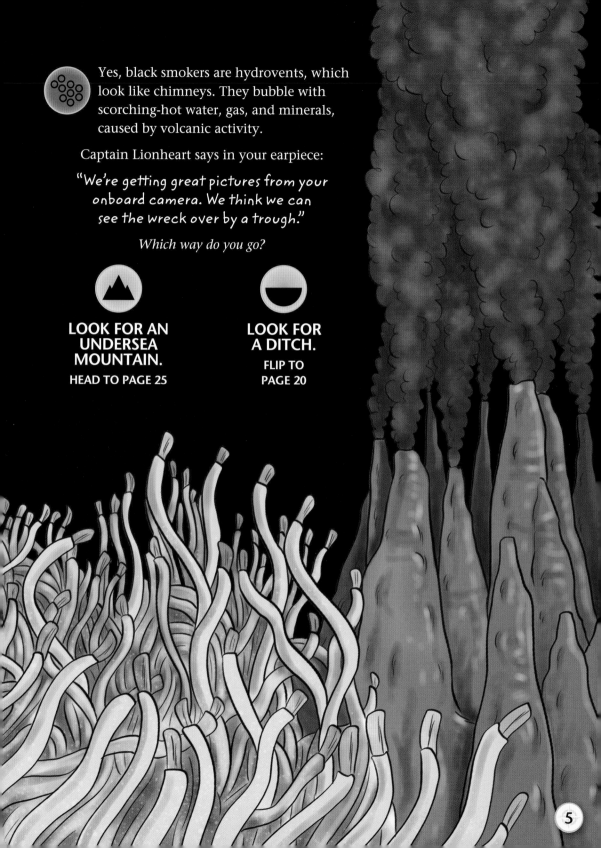

Yes, black smokers are hydrovents, which look like chimneys. They bubble with scorching-hot water, gas, and minerals, caused by volcanic activity.

Captain Lionheart says in your earpiece:

"We're getting great pictures from your onboard camera. We think we can see the wreck over by a trough."

Which way do you go?

LOOK FOR AN UNDERSEA MOUNTAIN.
HEAD TO PAGE 25

LOOK FOR A DITCH.
FLIP TO PAGE 20

That's right. The sea wears away rocks and beaches—this is known as erosion. All the caves, arches, and stacks along this coast were made by erosion. These features can be dangerous for sailors.

The climber shouts down again:

Watch out for shifting sandbanks, too. This is also a coast of deposition.

Whatever does he mean by that?

WAVES HERE DROP MATERIAL ONTO BEACHES.
TURN TO PAGE 18

WAVES HERE ARE GOOD FOR SURFING.
GO TO PAGE 9

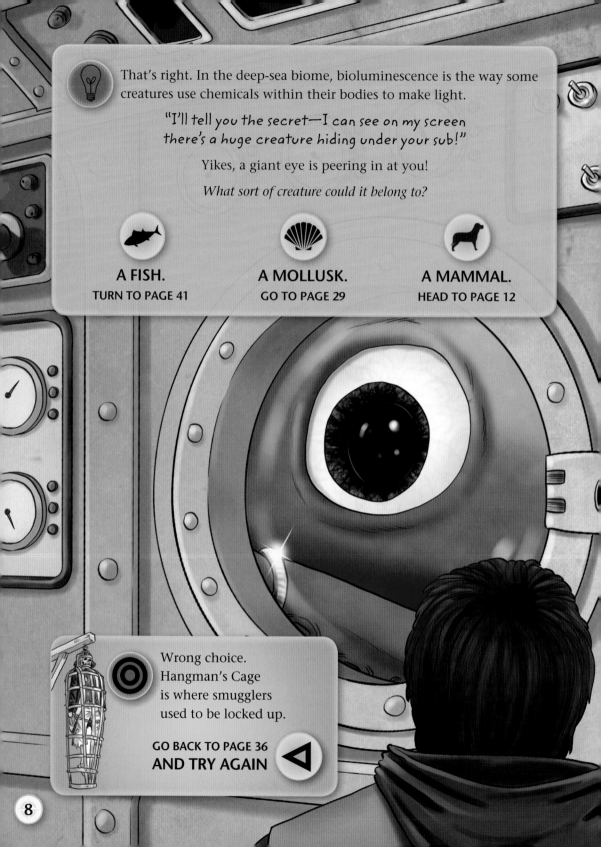

That's right. In the deep-sea biome, bioluminescence is the way some creatures use chemicals within their bodies to make light.

"I'll tell you the secret—I can see on my screen there's a huge creature hiding under your sub!"

Yikes, a giant eye is peering in at you!

What sort of creature could it belong to?

A FISH.

TURN TO PAGE 41

A MOLLUSK.

GO TO PAGE 29

A MAMMAL.

HEAD TO PAGE 12

Wrong choice. Hangman's Cage is where smugglers used to be locked up.

GO BACK TO PAGE 36 **AND TRY AGAIN**

No, the Arctic Ocean is the world's smallest ocean.

TURN BACK TO PAGE 41 AND TRY AGAIN 44,000

 No, that isn't what "deposition" means.

TURN BACK TO PAGE 6 AND TRY AGAIN

 That's right. A lighthouse is a tower with a powerful light at its top, which flashes to warn boats of dangerous rocks. A coastguard station has good views of the sea so that coastguards can keep a lookout for boats in trouble.

The lifeboat captain says:

"Remember it's a full moon tonight."

You scratch your head. How will that affect the sea?

THE WAVES WILL BE BIGGER.

HEAD TO PAGE 42

THE TIDES WILL BE STRONGER.

GO TO PAGE 37

 No, a gyre is not a storm.

TURN BACK TO PAGE 14 AND GUESS AGAIN

 Yes, that's right. The Pacific Ocean is the largest ocean, covering more than 30% of Earth's surface. You check the map. There's the island, just to your south: "Pacific Island."

As you pass the island, a speedboat comes racing toward you. The crew look scary—could they be pirates? The meanest-looking one leaps aboard and ties you to the mast!

Hand over your valuables . . . or else.

You explain you've got nothing worth stealing; you're just a geographer.

Prove it. I'll ask you three tough questions about this ocean. If you can answer them all, I'll set you free. Question one: This area is known as the Doldrums. What's that?

AN AREA WITH STRONG OCEAN CURRENTS.
GO TO PAGE 21

AN AREA OF OCEAN WITH HARDLY ANY WIND.
TURN TO PAGE 39

Wrong answer!

GO BACK TO PAGE 14
AND TRY AGAIN

That's right. A "sea snake" is a floating wave-power device to make electricity on the ocean surface from waves moving it up and down.

"Before I let you sail on your way," the lifeboat captain shouts, "answer me one question so I know you can be trusted alone out here."

"Why is this now called the Green Coast?"

IT PRODUCES CLEAN ENERGY.

GO TO PAGE 13

 IT FARMS SEAWEED.

FLIP TO PAGE 27

 ITS WATER IS GREEN FROM MINERALS.

HEAD TO PAGE 30

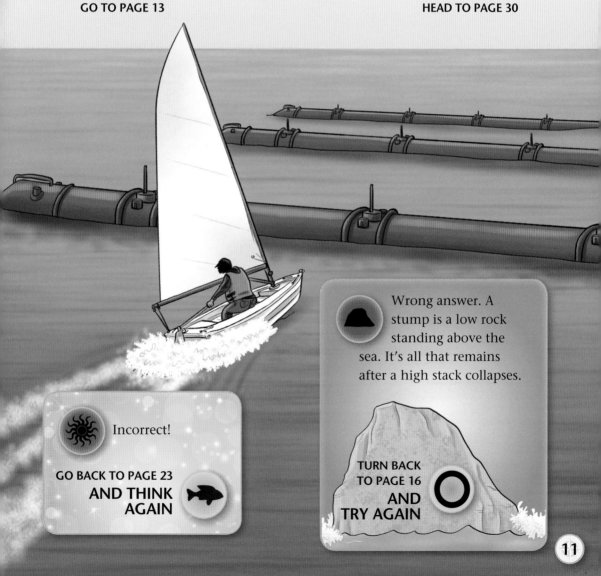

Wrong answer. A stump is a low rock standing above the sea. It's all that remains after a high stack collapses.

TURN BACK TO PAGE 16 **AND TRY AGAIN**

Incorrect!

GO BACK TO PAGE 23 **AND THINK AGAIN**

WANTED
CAPTAIN FLINTLOCK

 "The captain of the Shiver Me Timbers was a ruthless pirate called Flintlock. When his ship sank, he went down with it. To keep his voyages secret, he disguised all the place names in his log. But we do know he set sail from somewhere along the very coast on which my museum lies."

You turn to the first page of the logbook.

March 6, 1715

We set sail from a bay called Smuggler's Cove.

It looks like Flintlock dripped seawater on the word to make his directions harder to follow.

Which local feature is a bay?

SMUGGLER'S CAVE.
TURN TO PAGE 19

SMUGGLER'S COVE.
GO TO PAGE 26

SMUGGLER'S CURVE.
HEAD TO PAGE 23

---

61 Wrong answer!

GO BACK TO PAGE 24 AND TRY AGAIN

 Wrong! No mammals have eyes this huge.

GO BACK TO PAGE 8 AND TRY AGAIN

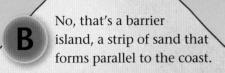

B No, that's a barrier island, a strip of sand that forms parallel to the coast.

GO BACK TO PAGE 33 AND RETHINK

 Wrong answer.

GO BACK TO PAGE 40 AND TRY AGAIN

That's right. Wave and tidal power are "green" energy because they are cleaner for the planet than burning fuel to make electricity. The lifeboat zooms off.

Suddenly you hear the coastguard calling on your radio:

Listen up, sailor! The wind is strengthening. We're expecting fierce westerlies.

So which direction will the wind be blowing?

IT WILL BLOW FROM THE WEST.
FLIP TO PAGE 42

IT WILL BLOW TO THE WEST.
TURN TO PAGE 39

You're exactly right! Seven on the Beaufort scale is a near gale, blowing up high frothy waves. But you're a good sailor on a sturdy yacht, so you should cope. The coastguard wishes you good luck.

Whooaaa! You battle the wind and waves all night. As the sun rises on the horizon, the gale at last dies down. You are emptying the water from your shoes when the coastguard calls on the radio again.

Give me your position. Were you pulled off course by the gyre?

What's a gyre?

A VERY POWERFUL STORM.
HEAD TO PAGE 9

A ROTATING OCEAN CURRENT.
TURN TO PAGE 24

A TIDAL WAVE.
FLICK TO PAGE 10

 No, don't panic—there's no monster.

TURN BACK TO PAGE 37 AND TRY AGAIN

 No, scientists haven't reported that the sun is getting much hotter.

TURN BACK TO PAGE 31 AND TRY AGAIN 71

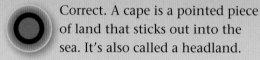

Correct. A cape is a pointed piece of land that sticks out into the sea. It's also called a headland.

You sail around the cape, flicking over the page to the next logbook entry:

"*Sailed close by the rocky ST✸✸✸.*"

Ahead of you is a limestone pillar, jutting out of the sea. Could the logbook mean that?

What is a rock like that called?

STACK.
HEAD TO PAGE 30

STUMP.
GO TO PAGE 11

 No, below 500 feet beneath the ocean surface, there's no light at all.

TURN BACK TO PAGE 40 AND TRY AGAIN

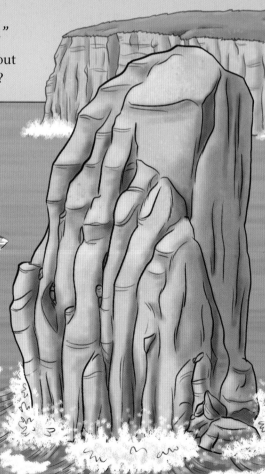

That's right. A tsunami is a huge wave that can cause terrible damage. Earthquakes or volcanic eruptions under the ocean can cause tsunamis.

Suddenly the boats are lifted on a massive wave, tossing the pirates into the sea. You are safe because you're still tied to the mast! But that wasn't a tsunami: the wave was made by a blue whale slapping its tail! You untie yourself and throw the screaming pirates an inflatable life raft.

You turn to the last entry in Captain Flintlock's logbook:

Since scraping over the atoll, we have sailed south for 4 hours. We are taking on water fast and I must make safe this log before ✵

Captain Flintlock never finished his entry.

TURN TO PAGE 19

TO FIND CAPTAIN FLINTLOCK'S WRECK

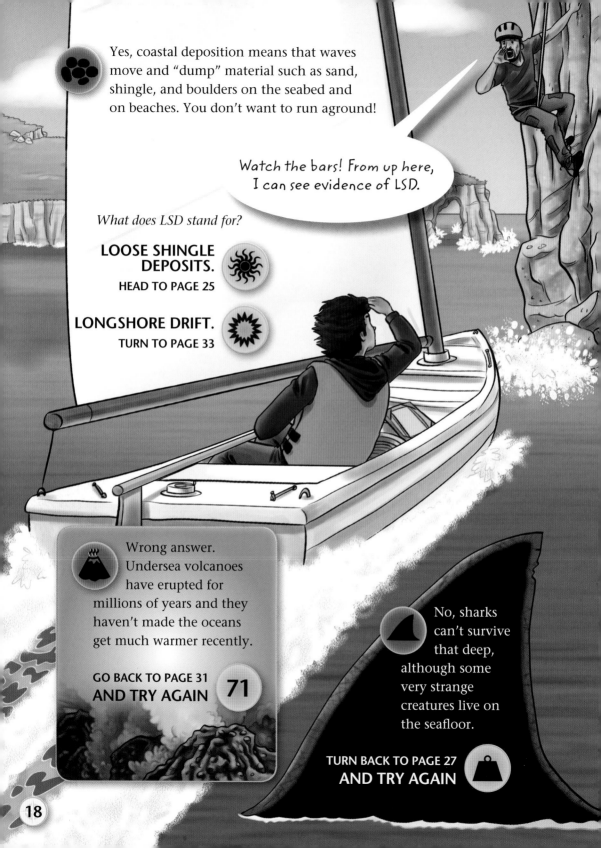

Yes, coastal deposition means that waves move and "dump" material such as sand, shingle, and boulders on the seabed and on beaches. You don't want to run aground!

Watch the bars! From up here, I can see evidence of LSD.

What does LSD stand for?

LOOSE SHINGLE DEPOSITS.
HEAD TO PAGE 25

LONGSHORE DRIFT.
TURN TO PAGE 33

Wrong answer. Undersea volcanoes have erupted for millions of years and they haven't made the oceans get much warmer recently.

GO BACK TO PAGE 31
AND TRY AGAIN 71

No, sharks can't survive that deep, although some very strange creatures live on the seafloor.

TURN BACK TO PAGE 27
AND TRY AGAIN

To calculate the spot where *Shiver Me Timbers* sank, you need to know your current position, which your instruments tell you is 11° North latitude and 142° East longitude.

But where exactly is 11° North, 142° East?

THE BERMUDA TRIANGLE.

FLIP TO PAGE 31

THE GREAT BARRIER REEF.

TURN TO PAGE 20

OVER THE MARIANA TRENCH.

GO TO PAGE 28

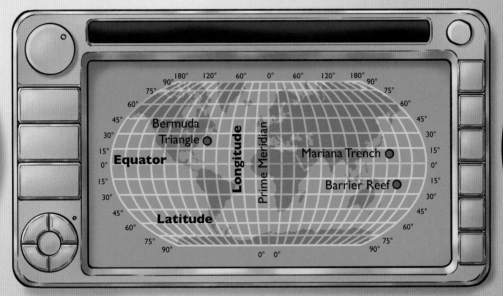

CLUE: Latitude lines on maps pinpoint places north or south of the equator. Longitude lines give the position east or west of the prime meridian.

Incorrect. A cave isn't a bay: it's a chamber cut into cliffs by pounding ocean waves.

TURN BACK TO PAGE 12 **AND TRY AGAIN**

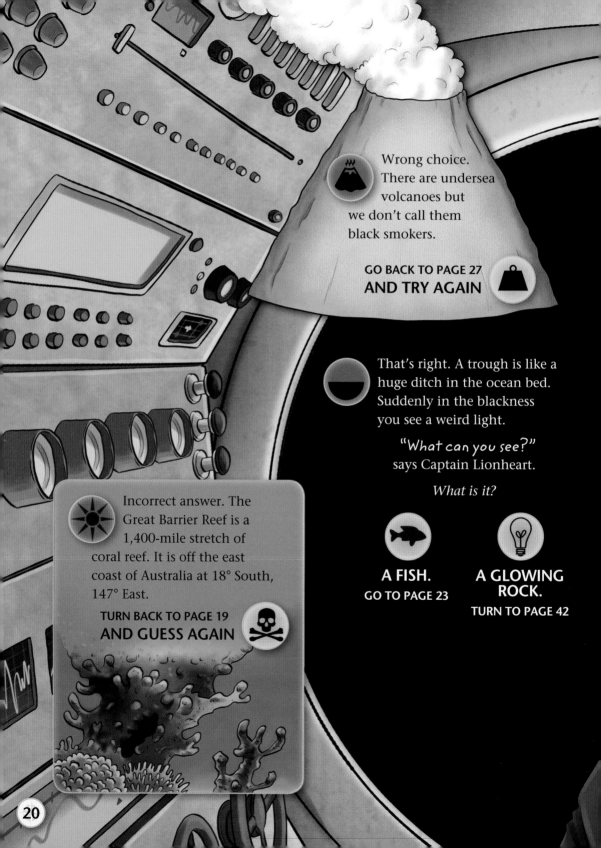

Wrong choice. There are undersea volcanoes but we don't call them black smokers.

GO BACK TO PAGE 27
AND TRY AGAIN

That's right. A trough is like a huge ditch in the ocean bed. Suddenly in the blackness you see a weird light.

"What can you see?" says Captain Lionheart.

What is it?

A FISH.
GO TO PAGE 23

A GLOWING ROCK.
TURN TO PAGE 42

Incorrect answer. The Great Barrier Reef is a 1,400-mile stretch of coral reef. It is off the east coast of Australia at 18° South, 147° East.

TURN BACK TO PAGE 19
AND GUESS AGAIN

No, harbors and docks aren't a sign of danger. A harbor is where boats can shelter or load and unload. Docks are harbors with specially built sea walls.

TURN BACK TO PAGE 22
AND TRY AGAIN C

❄ Incorrect.

**GO BACK TO PAGE 28
AND THINK AGAIN**

The pirate sneers in your face. "You're wasting time so think again, shipmate!"

TURN BACK TO PAGE 10
**AND DO WHAT
HE SAYS**

C That's right. A tombolo is a spit of sand and shingle that joins an island to the mainland. It is formed by longshore drift.

As you turn southeast and out to sea, a lifeboat motors through the waves toward you.

The captain is shouting at you.

There's a storm brewing so be careful. They used to call this coast the "sailors' graveyard." Just look at the shore! Those buildings show there used to be a lot of wrecks here.

Which buildings?

THE LIGHTHOUSE AND COASTGUARD STATION.
GO TO PAGE 9

THE HARBOR AND DOCKS.
TURN TO PAGE 21

That's right: it's an anglerfish. In the dark of the deep ocean, its light attracts smaller creatures toward it . . . so it can gobble them up!

"If you can answer a question, I'll tell you a secret," chuckles Captain Lionheart.

"What's the word for the way deep-sea creatures make light?"

BIORADIANCE.
GO TO PAGE 36

BIOGLIMMER.
HEAD TO PAGE 11

BIOLUMINESCENCE.
TURN TO PAGE 8

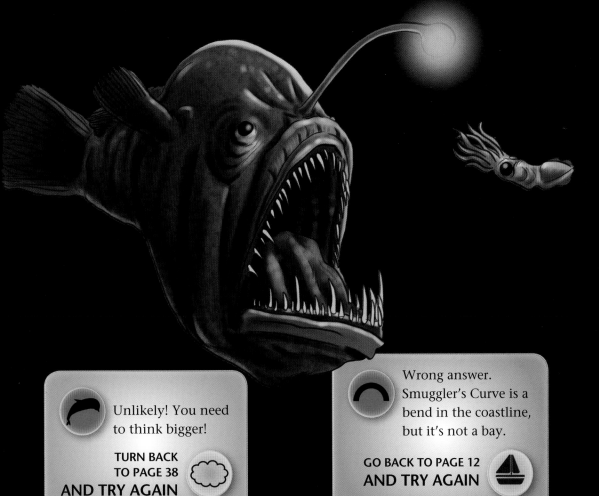

Unlikely! You need to think bigger!

TURN BACK TO PAGE 38
AND TRY AGAIN

Wrong answer. Smuggler's Curve is a bend in the coastline, but it's not a bay.

GO BACK TO PAGE 12
AND TRY AGAIN

Exactly right. Gyres are huge, circling movements of water—ocean currents thousands of miles across. There's a large one right around here but luckily you're still on course.

You check Captain Flintlock's logbook.

It's been mighty choppy lately and we're all seasick.

After 40 nautical miles, we turned southward.

You calculate that it's time for you to turn south, too.

Grrrrr! Your stomach's grumbling—but you're running out of provisions. Luckily, you can see a vessel on the horizon.

As you sail closer, a woman on board shouts:

Welcome to Ocean Lab, our floating laboratory where we study the oceans and the pollution that threatens them.

I'm Professor Strick. You're welcome aboard if you can answer this question. What is the percentage of Earth's surface that is covered by oceans?

51

51%.

GO TO
PAGE 43

61

61%.

TURN TO
PAGE 12

71

71%.

HEAD TO
PAGE 31

Wrong answer. We *are* talking about deposits of shingle and sand, but that's not the correct term.

TURN BACK TO PAGE 18 AND TRY AGAIN

You're as silly as a sausage!

TURN BACK TO PAGE 32 AND TRY AGAIN

Wrong answer. A tidal turbine is a machine that makes electricity from the moving water of the tides. A "sea snake" does something else.

TURN BACK TO PAGE 37 AND TRY AGAIN

4,400 Afraid not.

GO BACK TO PAGE 43 AND TRY AGAIN

No, an undersea mountain is called a seamount, not a trough.

TURN BACK TO PAGE 5 AND THINK AGAIN

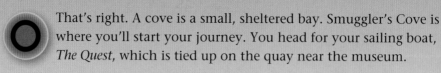

That's right. A cove is a small, sheltered bay. Smuggler's Cove is where you'll start your journey. You head for your sailing boat, *The Quest*, which is tied up on the quay near the museum.

Oops . . . the harbor mistress is standing by your boat.

You forgot to sign in at my office when you tied up. Now pay me a fine or you'll go nowhere today!

You explain that you're a geographer on an urgent mission to Smuggler's Cove.

If what you say is true, you'll know which direction to take to reach the cove.

Smuggler's Cove

N

W

E

S

Ocean Explorers Museum

Get out your compass. Which direction is the cove?

WESTSOUTH.
TURN TO PAGE 28

SOUTH.
GO TO PAGE 31

WEST.
HEAD TO PAGE 36

Captain Lionheart is impressed you know that the water pressure on the ocean floor will be like having a stack of jumbo jets on top of you. Luckily, the submarine is extra strong.

You climb into the sub and the crew lowers you into the sea.
You descend, down, down, down . . .

"Watch out for black smokers on the seabed!"
says Captain Lionheart through your radio earpiece.

Yikes, what are black smokers?

KILLER SHARKS.
GO TO PAGE 18

BUBBLING VENTS.
TURN TO PAGE 5

UNDERSEA VOLCANOES.
HEAD TO PAGE 20

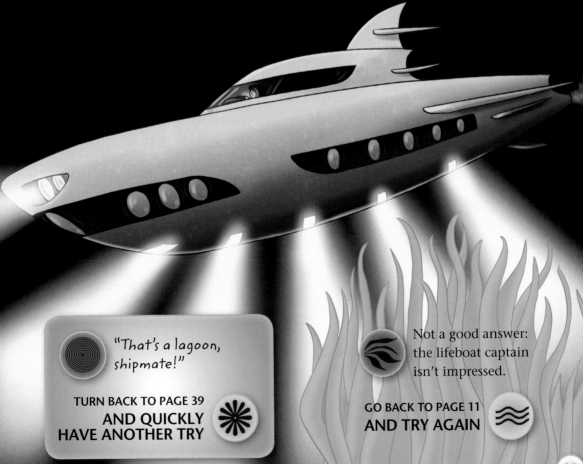

"That's a lagoon, shipmate!"

TURN BACK TO PAGE 39
AND QUICKLY HAVE ANOTHER TRY

Not a good answer: the lifeboat captain isn't impressed.

GO BACK TO PAGE 11
AND TRY AGAIN

There's no such direction: it should be "southwest." "North" or "south" always comes first when giving compass directions.

TURN BACK TO PAGE 26 AND THINK AGAIN

440 That wasn't right.

TURN BACK TO PAGE 43 AND CHOOSE AGAIN

That's right. The Mariana Trench is in the Pacific Ocean. It's the deepest part of the Earth's oceans, making it the deepest place on Earth.

You sail south while your onboard computer calculates the location of the wreck. You radio the Navy your final position and ask to borrow a deep-sea submarine.

They radio back:

But you're over a subduction zone! You can only use our submarine if you know what that means.

What is a subduction zone?

WHERE ONE PART OF THE SEABED IS PUSHED BELOW ANOTHER.
GO TO PAGE 40

WHERE ROCKS UNDER THE SEABED FREEZE.
TURN TO PAGE 21

That's right. It's a giant squid. A mollusk is an animal with a soft body and no backbone. The largest mollusk is the giant squid, which has eyes the size of soccer balls so it can see in the dark.

One of the giant squid's tentacles is wearing a glinting bracelet! The creature shoots off and you follow at full speed. It darts into its lair.

At last! You can see the wreck—and poor Captain Flintlock's skeleton. A chest is perched dangerously on the edge of an abyss. You carefully extend the submarine's robotic grippers. If you knock the chest off, it will be lost forever because even your sub can't descend that deep. Your hands tremble as the grippers grab the chest . . . just as the skeleton plunges into the abyss.

Take the chest back
to the surface.

TURN TO PAGE 34

**TO FIND OUT
WHAT'S IN IT**

Correct answer. A stack is a high rock left standing in the sea after waves have worn away the land around it.

As you pass the stack, a rock climber calls down to you.

There are dangerous rocks around here. It's all because of erosion, so watch out!

Watch out for what?
What's erosion?

DANGEROUS TIDES AND CURRENTS.
GO TO PAGE 33

A NATURAL PROCESS THAT WEARS AWAY ROCKS.
HEAD TO PAGE 6

WIND AND RAIN STORMS.
TURN TO PAGE 36

Wrong! The water is definitely blue.

TURN BACK TO PAGE 11
AND CHOOSE AGAIN

Yes, the oceans cover 71% of Earth's surface and contain 97% of the planet's water.

The docking bay door opens and you sail inside. You ask if you could stock up on water and food.

Professor Strick answers:

If you can answer this question, I'll let you stock up. Why are the oceans getting warmer?

THE SUN IS GETTING HOTTER.
TURN TO PAGE 16

MORE GREENHOUSE GASES ARE IN THE ATMOSPHERE.
GO TO PAGE 38

MORE VOLCANOES ARE ERUPTING UNDER THE SEA.
HEAD TO PAGE 18

No, that would take you out to sea.

GO BACK TO PAGE 26 AND GUESS AGAIN

Wrong answer. The Bermuda Triangle area of mystery is where many boats and planes have been reported missing. It is in the Atlantic Ocean, at 25° North, 71° West.

TURN BACK TO PAGE 19 AND TRY AGAIN

That's right! A coral reef is a rocky ridge made up of the tiny skeletons of sea creatures. A ring of these coral islands is called an atoll.

The pirate laughs in your face.

Get my last question right or it's all over for you! Question three: What's the Japanese word for a huge wave?

SALAMI.
TURN TO PAGE 25

ORIGAMI.
HEAD TO PAGE 41

TSUNAMI.
GO TO PAGE 17

Wrong answer. There may be dangerous tides here, but that's not what "erosion" means.

TURN BACK TO PAGE 30
AND ATTEMPT AGAIN

No, the Atlantic is the second largest ocean.

TURN BACK TO PAGE 41
AND TRY AGAIN

44,000

Correct. Longshore drift is the movement of sand and pebbles along the coast. Waves deposit them along beaches, islands, and offshore banks called bars.

You turn back to the logbook.

We passed the tombolo then steered southeast.

Longshore current

A

Bay

Lagoon

B

Bay

Beach

Island

C

Which feature is a tombolo?

A

A.

GO TO PAGE 38

B

B.

HEAD TO PAGE 13

C

C.

TURN TO PAGE 22

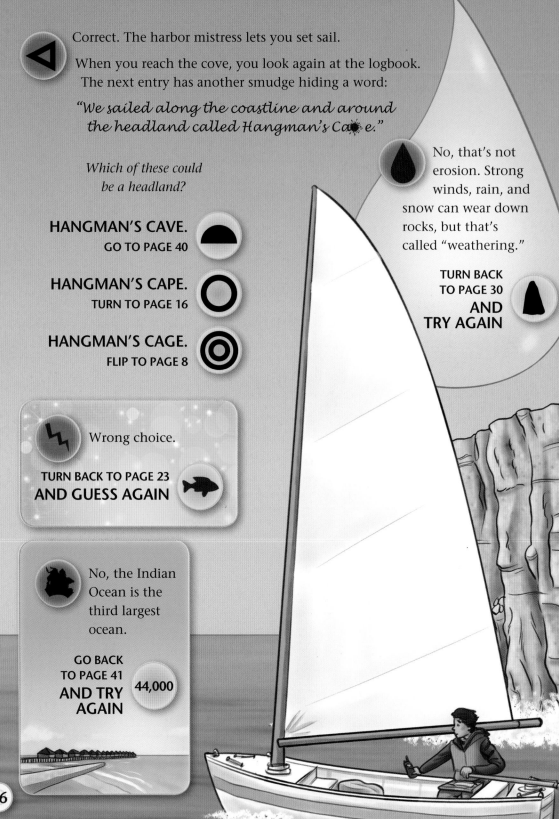

Correct. The harbor mistress lets you set sail.

When you reach the cove, you look again at the logbook. The next entry has another smudge hiding a word:

"We sailed along the coastline and around the headland called Hangman's Ca●e."

Which of these could be a headland?

HANGMAN'S CAVE.
GO TO PAGE 40

HANGMAN'S CAPE.
TURN TO PAGE 16

HANGMAN'S CAGE.
FLIP TO PAGE 8

No, that's not erosion. Strong winds, rain, and snow can wear down rocks, but that's called "weathering."

TURN BACK
TO PAGE 30
AND TRY AGAIN

Wrong choice.

TURN BACK TO PAGE 23
AND GUESS AGAIN

No, the Indian Ocean is the third largest ocean.

GO BACK
TO PAGE 41
AND TRY AGAIN

44,000

Yes, the moon affects the tides in Earth's oceans. The gravity force between the Earth and moon causes the regular rise and fall of the sea. During full and new moons, the gravity forces of the sun and moon combine to cause the highest tides, called spring tides.

You'd better watch out for the sea snake!

Yikes! Is there a sea monster?

YES, SAIL FOR THE SHORE—FAST!

HEAD TO PAGE 16

NO, IT'S A TIDAL TURBINE.

GO TO PAGE 25

NO, IT'S A WAVE-POWER DEVICE.

TURN TO PAGE 11

No, that's 11 on the Beaufort scale. That would be a violent storm with very high waves.

GO BACK TO PAGE 42
AND HAVE ANOTHER GUESS

No, the Southern Ocean is the fourth largest ocean.

FLIP BACK TO PAGE 41
AND TRY AGAIN

44,000

A No, that's a spit. A spit is a long stretch of sand and shingle formed by longshore drift. Spits often develop at the mouths of bays.

TURN BACK TO PAGE 33
AND THINK AGAIN

That's right. Over the past century, the burning of fuel and other human activities have released huge amounts of greenhouse gases. They trap heat in the atmosphere and raise temperatures, particularly in the oceans.

Professor Strick shows you a diagram of the greenhouse effect. She doesn't seem ready to hand over any food yet. She's got another question.

THE GREENHOUSE EFFECT

Some sunlight is reflected. Some becomes heat.

Carbon dioxide and other greenhouse gases trap heat, keeping the Earth warm.

"Do you know what effect the warmer oceans are having?"

HAPPIER DOLPHINS.
FLIP TO PAGE 23

HIGHER SEA LEVELS.
TURN TO PAGE 43

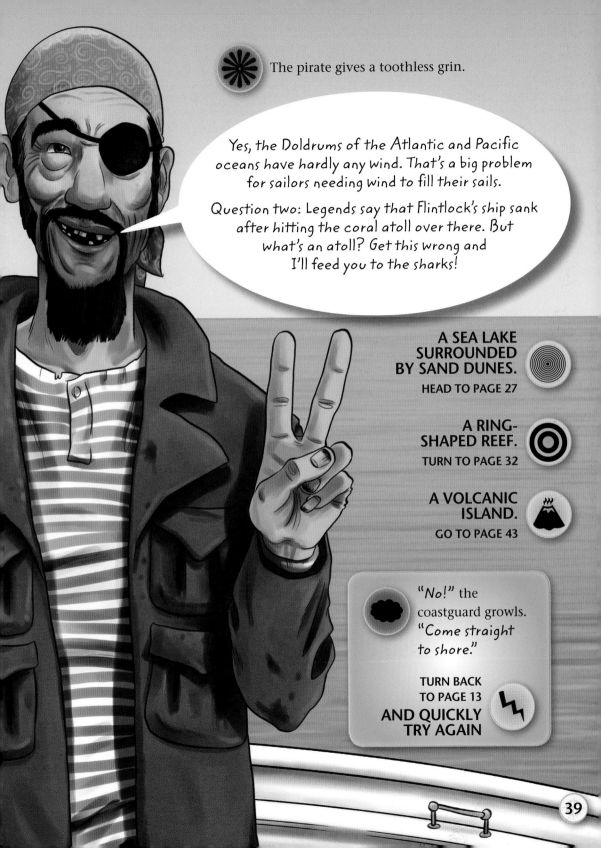

The pirate gives a toothless grin.

Yes, the Doldrums of the Atlantic and Pacific oceans have hardly any wind. That's a big problem for sailors needing wind to fill their sails.

Question two: Legends say that Flintlock's ship sank after hitting the coral atoll over there. But what's an atoll? Get this wrong and I'll feed you to the sharks!

A SEA LAKE SURROUNDED BY SAND DUNES.
HEAD TO PAGE 27

A RING-SHAPED REEF.
TURN TO PAGE 32

A VOLCANIC ISLAND.
GO TO PAGE 43

"*No!*" the coastguard growls. "*Come straight to shore.*"

TURN BACK TO PAGE 13 AND QUICKLY **TRY AGAIN**

Incorrect. Hangman's Cave is a chamber cut into the cliffs by the sea, so it isn't a headland.

TURN BACK TO PAGE 36 AND TRY AGAIN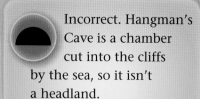

No, that's 12 on the Beaufort scale, which is as high as the scale goes. It would be a hurricane with massive waves.

TURN BACK TO PAGE 42 AND TRY AGAIN

Correct answer. The Mariana Trench is where two sections of Earth's crust (called tectonic plates) meet and one pushes below the other.

The Navy arrives and the crew hauls you aboard.
Captain Lionheart greets you.

You can use our sub if you convince me you know what you're doing. You're going to be under massive pressure down on the seabed. Do you know what that means?

YOU SHOULD TRY NOT TO BITE YOUR NAILS.
GO TO PAGE 13

YOU'LL HAVE A GREAT WEIGHT PRESSING DOWN ON YOU.
TURN TO PAGE 27

YOU'LL NEED DARK GLASSES—IT'S BRIGHT DOWN THERE.
HEAD TO PAGE 16

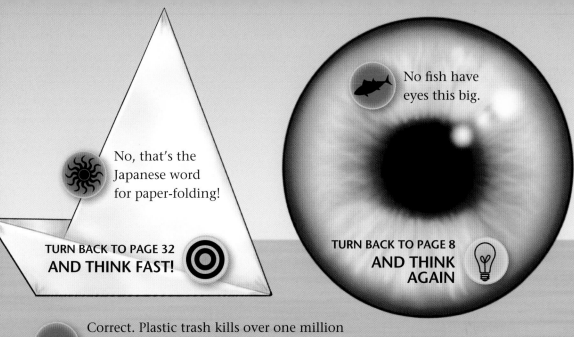

No, that's the Japanese word for paper-folding!

TURN BACK TO PAGE 32
AND THINK FAST!

No fish have eyes this big.

TURN BACK TO PAGE 8
AND THINK AGAIN

44,000 Correct. Plastic trash kills over one million sea birds, marine mammals, and other sea creatures each year.

The door swings open. Professor Strick helps you load up *The Quest* and waves good-bye. You look again at Captain Flintlock's logbook:

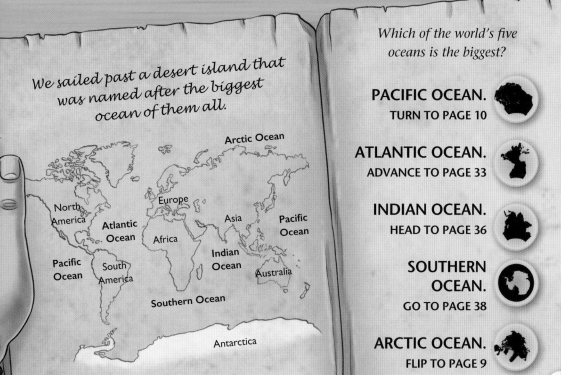

We sailed past a desert island that was named after the biggest ocean of them all.

Arctic Ocean

North America
Europe
Asia
Pacific Ocean
Atlantic Ocean
Africa
Pacific Ocean
South America
Indian Ocean
Australia
Southern Ocean
Antarctica

Which of the world's five oceans is the biggest?

PACIFIC OCEAN.
TURN TO PAGE 10

ATLANTIC OCEAN.
ADVANCE TO PAGE 33

INDIAN OCEAN.
HEAD TO PAGE 36

SOUTHERN OCEAN.
GO TO PAGE 38

ARCTIC OCEAN.
FLIP TO PAGE 9

Wrong answer. The wind causes waves to move up and down on the surface of the oceans. That has nothing to do with a full moon.

TURN BACK TO PAGE 9
AND THINK AGAIN

 No, there are no glowing deep-sea rocks.

TURN BACK TO PAGE 20
AND TRY AGAIN

Yes, I'm glad you know that winds are named after the direction from which they blow.

But can your yacht cope with the strength of the coming winds? We expect gusts of 7 on the Beaufort scale.

Do you need to head for the harbor? How fast are gusts of 7?

32–38 MILES PER HOUR.
GO TO PAGE 14

64–75 MILES PER HOUR.
TURN TO PAGE 37

OVER 76 MILES PER HOUR.
FLIP TO PAGE 40

51 No, think bigger.

**TURN BACK TO PAGE 24
AND HAVE
ANOTHER TRY**

"Wrong! Now walk the plank!"

**TURN BACK TO PAGE 39
AND THINK FAST**

That's right. Oceans are rising because water expands when it heats up. Warmer oceans also melt ice at the poles so more water is released into the sea. By 2100, many coastal cities could be flooded.

Professor Strick leads you to Ocean Lab's food storeroom.

I'll give you a clue to the entry code for the storeroom door: On average, how many pieces of plastic trash are in every square mile of ocean?

What's the entry code?

440.
GO TO PAGE 28   440

4,400.
TURN TO PAGE 25   4,400

44,000.
HEAD TO PAGE 41   44,000

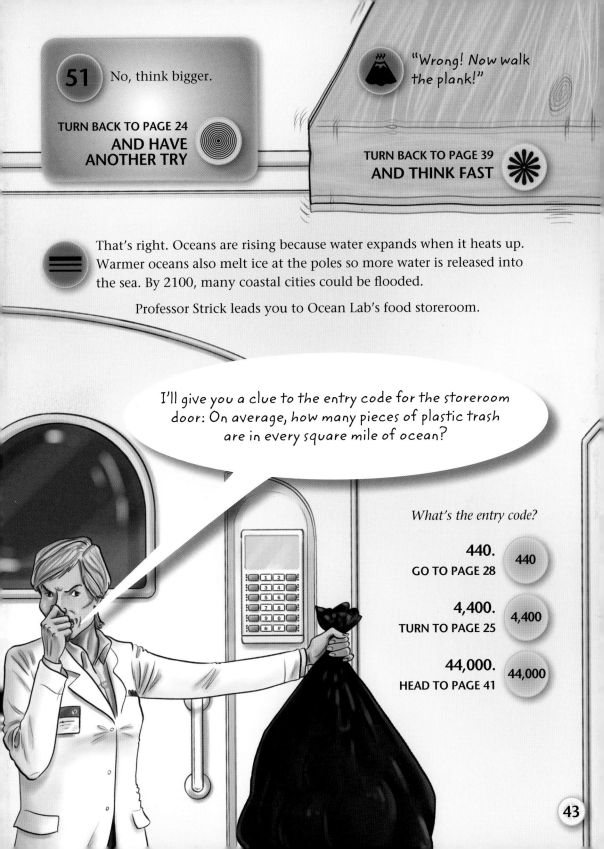

GLOSSARY

Abyss
A drop so deep, or a space so great, that it is almost impossible to measure.

Atoll
A ring-shaped reef (ridges of sand or rock near the water surface).

Bar
A sand bar is a long strip of deposited sand lying offshore. It is usually only exposed at low tide.

Bay
A curved space cut into a coastline, usually eroded into softer rocks. Bays often contain beaches and provide an area of shelter for boats and for settlements.

Beaufort scale
A scale from 0 to 12 to indicate the speed and strength of the wind.

Biome
A large area on Earth's surface, or in its oceans, with a particular habitat that suits the animals and plants living there.

Coastal deposition
When the sea drops material (such as sand and shingle) that it has been carrying.

Coastal erosion
The wearing away and removal of material by the force of the sea.

Coastguard
An officer of an organization that carries out search and rescue at sea. In some countries, coastguards also act as an ocean-going police force.

Coral reef
An offshore stretch of dead coral, usually with live coral (tiny sea animals in large colonies that live in warm, shallow, clear saltwater) on top.

Current

The continuous movement of seawater in a particular direction. Currents are created by forces such as wind and temperature.

Doldrums

A part of the ocean near the equator that is known as being calm, with no wind.

Equator

An imaginary circle around Earth at 0° latitude. It is equally distant from the North Pole and South Pole.

Greenhouse gas

A gas (such as carbon dioxide) that absorbs radiation and warms Earth's surface. This contributes to climate change.

Gyre

A large system of circling ocean currents. A gyre is often linked with large wind movements.

Harbor

An area of protected water that is deep enough to be a place of safety for ships.

Headland

An area of land jutting out into the sea that separates bays and coves.

Hydrovent

Also known as a hydrothermal vent. A hydrovent is a narrow opening in the deep-ocean floor from which bubbling, mineral-rich water rises. The water is heated within the Earth by volcanic activity.

Lagoon

A protected area of water between a barrier beach or coral reef and a coastline, or in the center of an atoll.

Latitude

A geographic coordinate that tells us how far north or south of the equator a point is.

Lifeboat

A boat used for rescuing people at sea. Lifeboats may be operated by the coastguard or a volunteer (unpaid) force.

Limestone
Solid rock formed from the deposited remains of sea creatures and sediments (such as sand and minerals) over millions of years.

Longitude
A geographic coordinate that tells us how far east or west of the prime meridian a point is.

Longshore drift
The movement of sediment (such as sand and shingle) along a coast. Material is pushed up a beach by waves, and across at the same time by the current, so that material steadily moves along the shore.

Mollusk
A group of animals (such as snails, clams, and octopuses) with a soft body and no skeleton. Mollusks are often enclosed in a shell.

Nautical mile
A unit of distance (one-sixtieth of a degree of latitude) used for sea navigation. A nautical mile is just over a land mile, at about 6,000 feet. Speed at sea is measured in knots: a knot is about one nautical mile per hour.

Plate tectonics
The slight movement of large sections of Earth's crust.

Pollution

The spoiling or contamination of the environment (air, water, or soil) by human activity.

Prime meridian

The 0° line of longitude running north to south, from which positions east and west are measured. The line runs through Greenwich in England.

Quay

A structure built along the bank of a waterway, used as a landing place for boats.

Tide

The regular rise and fall of sea levels. Tides are caused by the gravitational pulls of the sun and moon.

Tsunami

A great sea wave produced by an earthquake or volcanic eruption under the ocean.

Turbine

An engine for making energy, with a central driving shaft fitted with blades that are spun around by the pressure of water, steam, or air.

Volcano

A hill or mountain formed when material from inside Earth is forced out through an opening in the crust.

Taking it further

The Geography Quest books are designed to inspire children to develop and apply their geographical knowledge through compelling adventure stories. For each story, children must solve a series of problems and challenges on their way to completing an exciting quest.

The books do not follow a page-by-page order. The reader jumps forward and backward through the book according to the answers given to the problems. If his or her answers are correct, the reader progresses to the next part of the story; incorrect answers are fully explained before the reader is directed back to attempt the problem once again. Additional help can be found in the glossary at the back of the book.

To support the development of your child's geographical knowledge, you can:

⚓ Read the book with your child.

⚓ Solve the initial problems together and discover how the book works.

⚓ Continue reading with your child until he or she has understood how to follow the "Go to" instructions to the next puzzle or explanation, and is flipping through the book confidently.

⚓ Encourage your child to read on alone. Prompt your child to tell you how the story develops and what problems they have solved. Take the time to ask, "What's happening now?"

⚓ Point out the importance of oceans to our planet. On a local scale, the sea shapes coastlines and impacts on all manner of human activities. On a global scale, the oceans affect climate —and are affected by climate change. It is vital that we all respect and understand the power of the oceans, as well as marine habitats.

⚓ Discuss what it would be like if you could travel to the depths of the deepest oceans and what we might discover in this still largely unexplored region of Earth.

⚓ Most of all, make geography fun!